JOURNEY
into the
Arctic

Bryan and Cherry Alexander

OXFORD
UNIVERSITY PRESS

To Max and Jack

OXFORD
UNIVERSITY PRESS

Oxford New York

Auckland Bangkok Buenos Aires Cape Town Chennai
Dar es Salaam Delhi Hong Kong Istanbul Karachi Kolkata
Kuala Lumpur Madrid Melbourne Mexico City Mumbai Nairobi
São Paulo Shanghai Taipei Tokyo Toronto

Published by Oxford University Press, Inc.
198 Madison Avenue, New York, NY 10016
www.oup.com

Oxford is a registered trade mark of Oxford University Press, Inc.

Copyright © Bryan and Cherry Alexander 2003

Database right Oxford University Press (maker)

First published 2003

Library of Congress Cataloging-in-Publication Data is available.

Library ISBN 0-19-522004-8
Trade ISBN 0-19-522005-6

1 3 5 7 9 10 8 6 4 2

Printed in Hong Kong

Contents

Map of the
Journey

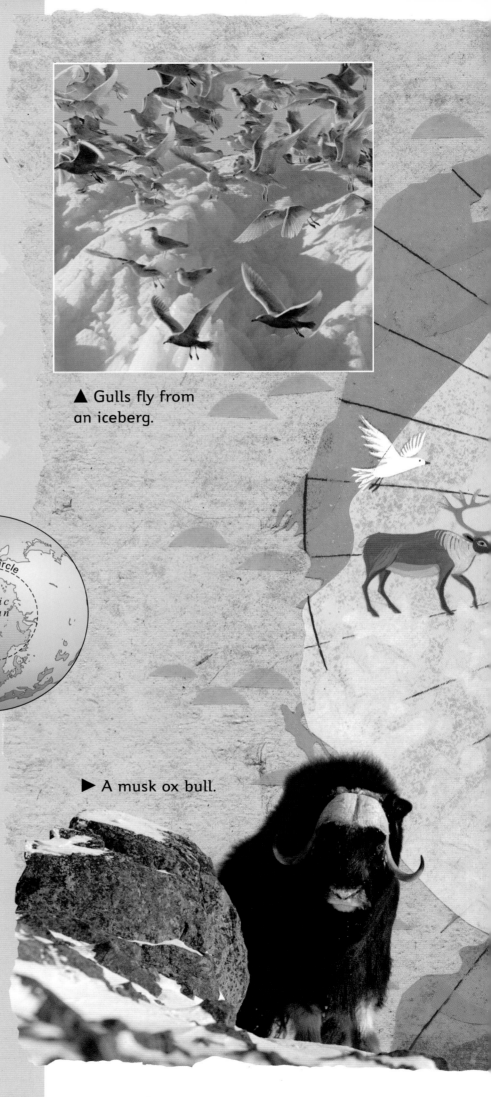

We are going to take a very long journey in the north. The Arctic is the area north of the Arctic Circle, which is an imaginary line on the globe. In the winter the Arctic is cold, and in the High Arctic the Sun sets in early November and does not rise again until the end of January. At this time, the sea freezes to a depth of more than three feet and the land is covered in snow. Everything is white, and some of the animals and birds have white fur or feathers for camouflage. In the summer the daytime temperatures are mostly above freezing, and the area is rich in wildlife.

We are going to start our trip in Greenland in winter after the return of the Sun. We will take a dogsled to Arctic Canada as the days lengthen, meeting polar bears and seeing icebergs. As winter turns to summer and flowers and birds make the most of the daylight, we reach Siberia to travel with reindeer herders. Then we join an icebreaker for the final part of the trip. Only by taking such a long journey through the seasons and across continents can we experience the full contrasts of life in the Arctic.

▲ Gulls fly from an iceberg.

► A musk ox bull.

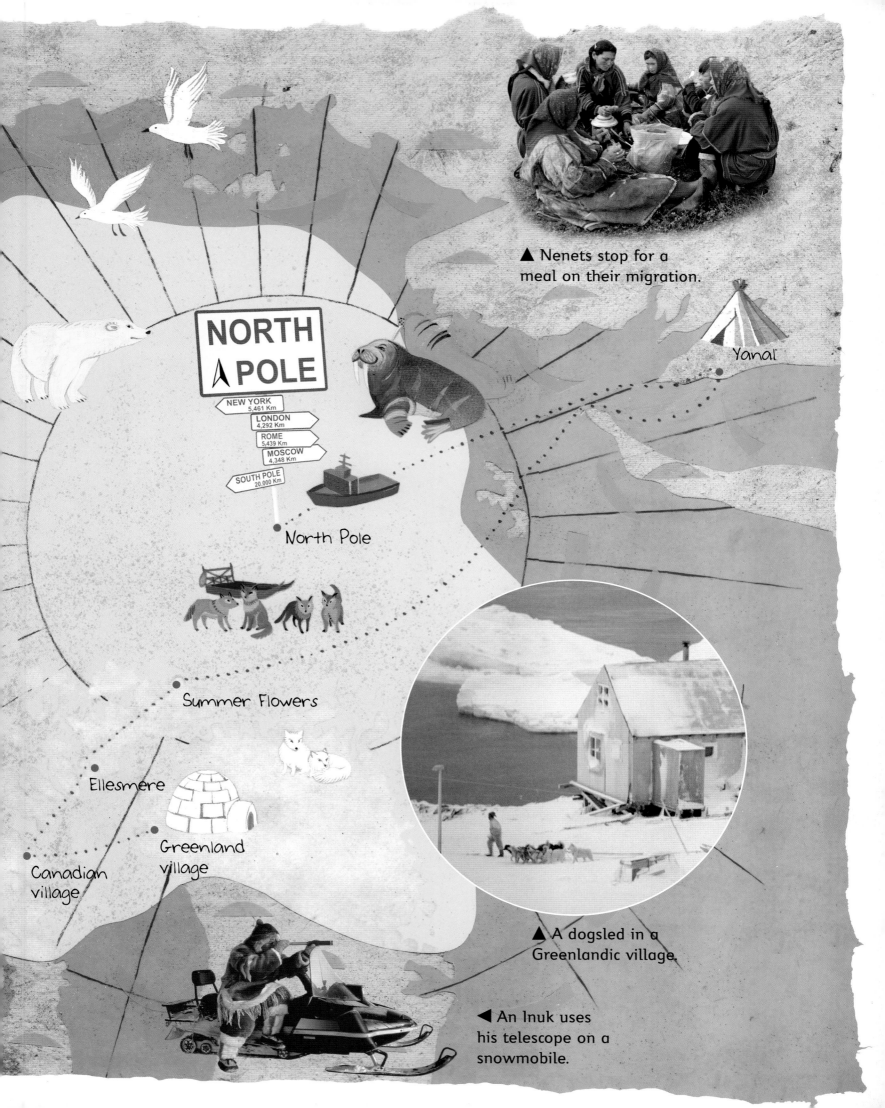

▲ Nenets stop for a meal on their migration.

NORTH ⬆ POLE

NEW YORK
5,461 Km

LONDON
4,292 Km

ROME
5,439 Km

MOSCOW
4,348 Km

SOUTH POLE
20,000 Km

Yanar

North Pole

Summer Flowers

Ellesmere

Greenland village

Canadian village

▲ A dogsled in a Greenlandic village.

◀ An Inuk uses his telescope on a snowmobile.

Be Prepared

▶ Clothes made for skiing or mountain-climbing trap air in the down and pile, so they keep us warm. But they are not as warm as furs.

Our journey in the Arctic will be an adventure, and although we will be taken good care of, we need to know how to keep warm even on the coldest days. The native people of the Arctic learned this from the animals that share their world. They dressed in the skins of the animals they hunted for food and found that they kept them very warm.

The secret is to trap layers of air—like the air in a fluffed-up down comforter—so tight clothing isn't much good. The fur of caribou or reindeer is always warm because the hair is hollow and traps the air. Sealskin is often used for boots and mittens because it is light and windproof. In North Greenland the men wear polar bear-skin trousers when out hunting because they are very warm and tough.

▼ Inuit children dressed in caribou-fur clothing.

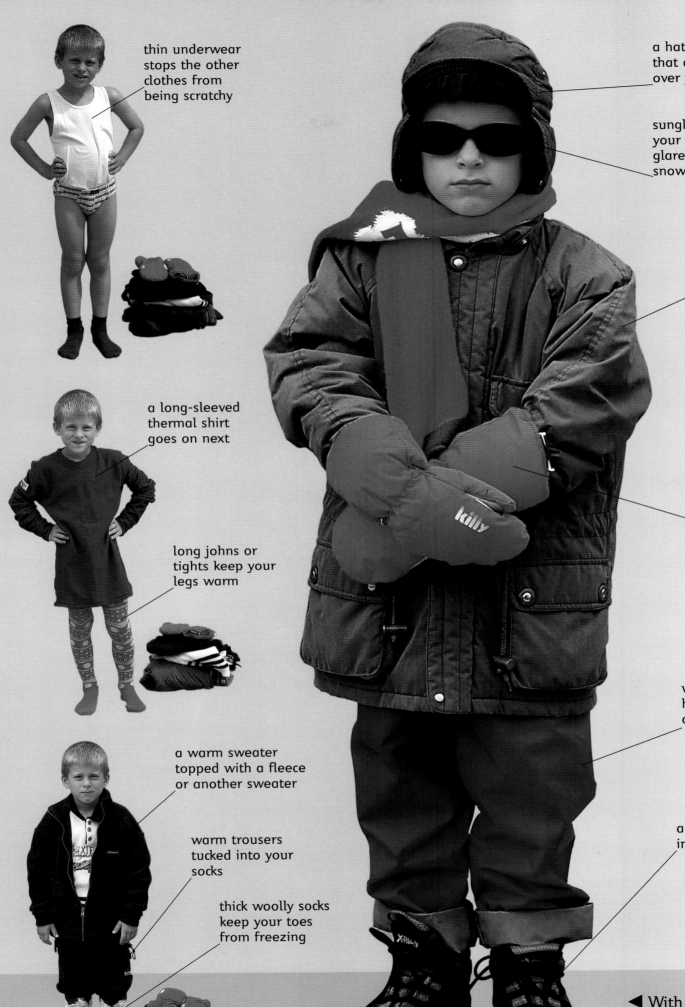

thin underwear stops the other clothes from being scratchy

a hat with flaps that can pull down over your ears

sunglasses to protect your eyes from the glare off the white snow and ice

a warm jacket padded with down or synthetic material

a long-sleeved thermal shirt goes on next

thick mittens worn over thinner gloves keep your fingers warm

long johns or tights keep your legs warm

waterproof trousers help to keep out the cold wind

a warm sweater topped with a fleece or another sweater

a roomy pair of insulated boots

warm trousers tucked into your socks

thick woolly socks keep your toes from freezing

◄ With so many clothes on, you will feel bulky but you will keep warm.

A Cold Start

The helicopter sets down outside a North Greenlandic village, and as the doors open we realize just how cold it is. All around everything is white. The little hairs in our noses freeze and feel stiff, and the snow squeaks as we walk on it. It is -22 degrees F. Half the village is here to meet the helicopter, which is bringing in mail and groceries.

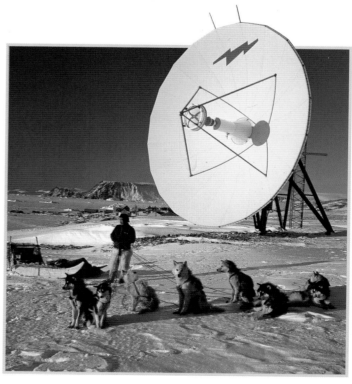

▲ The satellite dish is the village's link to the outside world, carrying television and telephone messages.

◄ An Inuit hunter leads his dog team and sled along the shore. Huge icebergs float in the water.

A man steps forward. He is Mamarut, our guide for the first part of our journey. He is warmly dressed in furs, but most of the villagers are in ordinary clothes. Lots of children are running about. Mamarut lives in a wooden house by the beach, but the sea is frozen, with huge icebergs in it.

▲ Warmly dressed Inuit girls play on a toboggan in the snow.

Life here is a mix of the modern and the traditional. We will be riding on a wooden sled pulled by a team of husky dogs, similar to those used in this area for hundreds of years, but inside many of the houses it is warm and comfortable, with television, video, and many of the things we have at home.

This far north the Sun sets for the winter in early November and rises again at the end of January. Now, in March, it rises a little higher in the sky each day, but it is still very cold. While Mamarut harnesses all his huskies to the sled, we put on our warmest clothes. Once we are all aboard the sled Mamarut cracks his whip, says "huk, huk" to his dog team, and we race off across the sea ice, heading west.

◄ Mamarut's warm clothes are made of fur from polar bear, sheep, and arctic fox.

A Secretive
Seal

After a racing start the huskies settle down to a steady pace. They pant with the heat of running, even though it is so cold. After a while Mamarut points out a small hole in the sea ice. What is it for? We get down from the sled to take a closer look.

It's a seal's breathing hole, one of several that the seal must keep open all winter. He needs the hole to come up to breathe, and he must have several because if there is a polar bear waiting at one, he will have to use another. Even though by the end of winter the ice is more than a yard thick, the seal keeps the holes open with his teeth and the claws on his front flippers. Mamarut signals us to stand very still. He takes the dogs a short way off, so the seal will think we have all left.

▼ The huskies are curled up asleep as the low rays of the Sun shine on the snow ridges.

These ridges in the snow are cut by the wind. They are called sastrugi.

We are waiting for the seal to come back to this hole to breathe. Any noise we make on the crunchy snow will be magnified under the water, and he will think someone is waiting to eat him. This is a ringed seal, the most common seal in the far north. They have learned to live under the sea ice all through the winter. After several minutes we hear the soft sound of a seal breathing! We might just glimpse his sensitive whiskers at the bottom of his hole—but one of us crunches some snow by mistake and we hear a sharp intake of breath, then silence. The seal has gone. It is time for us to leave too, we have a long way to go.

▼ Young ringed seals like this one are hunted by both people and polar bears.

Meet the
Polar Bear

We travel for days across the frozen sea, always westward. The huskies seem tireless, and we get used to sleeping in a tent over the dogsled. One morning Mamarut points out some tracks in the snow. They were made by a polar bear mother and two cubs.

Looking ahead, we can see shapes on the snow some distance away. We stop the sled and wait to see what the bears will do. The wind is blowing our scent away, and the mother comes closer to get a good look at us, trying to decide what we are. A good predator is always curious, and will check out anything that is different just in case it is edible.

▲ An Inuit hunter looks closely at polar bear tracks to see how fresh they are.

▼ Two polar bear cubs, safely behind their mother, peek over her back.

Also having two hungry mouths to feed must be keeping the mother busy. She is careful to keep her cubs behind her in case we are a threat to them. When she is still a safe distance away, she stops. Mamarut has checked that his gun is within reach, but he doesn't need to use it. She has realized that we are not going to be their next meal. Perhaps they have eaten recently, because the family stops in the snow and the cubs start to play, tugging on her ears and running at each other. When they all settle down together in the snow to rest, we continue on our way, leaving without disturbing them.

▶ Polar bears are solitary animals and hunt alone, except when they have cubs.

▲ The fan shape of the huskies' ropes is good for traveling on sea ice.

Icebergs and the
Arctic Fox

We are not the only ones to find the polar bear tracks. Almost immediately we see an arctic fox looking at them. In the winter, arctic foxes find it hard to hunt for food and will often follow a polar bear to clean up his leftovers. The bear isn't always pleased to be sharing his meal and will chase after the uninvited guest, so the fox is very careful.

As we get nearer, the fox decides to follow the tracks later, and runs lightly across the snow, looking almost like a small ball of white fur blown in the wind. He hides behind a small iceberg. We won't see him again. Mamarut takes this chance to untangle his dogs. Each husky is joined to the sled with a rope about 12 feet long. Ideally they should run side by side, but in fact they like to run beside friends, and keep jumping over the ropes to get to different positions.

◀ Two arctic foxes sniff the tracks of a polar bear in the snow.

▶ An Inuk untangles the ropes of his huskies, while the dogs sit patiently.

After an hour or so the lines are tangled and iced up, and they have to be untangled. Mamarut always does this. He takes off his mittens and works as quickly as he can in the cold air. The dogs take this chance to take a rest and eat some snow to cool off. When the ropes are straight again, we continue on our way, looking over our shoulders to see if we can spot the arctic fox returning to the polar bear tracks.

◀ Its fluffy white coat keeps this small arctic fox warm in the extreme cold.

The word "igloo" means house in the Inuit language and it is the word they use for any building. Their word for a snow house is "iglluviga." First Mamarut cuts the big blocks of snow, taking care to cut them from an area that will become the floor. The other half of the inside will be a sleeping platform—made of snow! He starts to build the lower level, sloping the sides of the blocks with his huge snow knife.

◀ Cutting the snow blocks with a saw. The type of snow must be just right.

Building an
Igloo

T he winter days are short, and as the skies turn pink with the setting Sun Mamarut takes a saw from his sled. He checks that the snow is deep and firm enough, then announces he is going to build an igloo! The Inuit no longer live in igloos, but they do sometimes use them as overnight shelters when they are traveling.

As the walls grow higher he needs to slope them in, so that he can place the blocks that will form the roof. When he comes to cut the opening for the door, he keeps it as low as possible. Warm air rises, so the warmth from our bodies and the stove will be trapped inside. If the door is too high, this precious warm air will escape into the freezing night.

► As the Sun sets, the huskies settle down to sleep outside, in their own fur coats.

Once Mamarut has finished the igloo he calls us to help him to pack the spaces between the bricks with snow, so no drafts can get in. Finally, as it gets really dark, we carry the reindeer skins inside, spread them out on the sleeping platform and light the pressure lamp. After a warming stew of seal meat, we are soon sleeping safe and snug beneath a roof of snow.

▼ The light from the pressure lamp glows through the snow bricks.

In Search of the
Right Ice

Next morning we wake early. It is eerily quiet out here. Everyone is longing for a hot drink, so Mamarut sends us off to collect some ice to melt for water. We return with a full kettle, boil it on the Primus stove and pour it into mugs with tea bags. Yuk! The tea is salty and horrible. Mamarut explains that there are two main types of ice around us, and we have collected the wrong one.

◄ Frost flowers form on thin sea ice and are very delicate.

Mamarut takes us over to a small iceberg, where he shows us how the ice looks clearer and breaks more cleanly than sea ice, which has salt in it.

The sea ice is made when the sea freezes in winter. At first it freezes flat over the sea, then it goes through several stages, including making pretty frost flowers. Winter winds can pile up the ice into high peaks, which look like icebergs. This is what we collected.

Real iceberg ice, however, is formed when snow falls high up in the mountains on icecaps and glaciers. There is no salt in it, and as more and more snow falls the weight of it forces the air out from between the snow flakes, making ice. This ice then starts to flow slowly downhill. Thousands of years later it reaches the sea, breaks off and floats away as an iceberg. We can see icebergs all around us, frozen into the sea ice.

▲ An Inuit boy climbs to the top of a small iceberg. Its sides are very steep and slippery.

This time we collect ice from a freshwater iceberg, and while the kettle boils we take turns sliding down a wonderful steep iceberg we have found. Its sides are smooth and we land in piles of soft snow. Mamarut calls us over to the sled. He has made us hot chocolate, which tastes much better than salty tea!

◄ An Inuk untangles his dog ropes in front of a large iceberg frozen into the sea ice.

Village
and Snowmobile

We have traveled so far with Mamarut that we are now in the Canadian Arctic, and he needs to go home. We began our journey in spring, and now it is early summer and much warmer. On our last day with Mamarut we come to a village.

◀ A young Inuit from Canada, wearing a fur-trimmed hood.

▲ A street in spring in a Canadian Inuit village. The thaw has already begun.

This is much bigger than the village in Greenland. It has a proper airport and several stores, and people are driving snowmobiles in the street. Mamarut takes us to the home of his friend Malliki, who will be our guide on the next stage of our journey.

We go into the large store to buy supplies for the trip. We will be traveling on a sled behind a snowmobile, so we will need to take enough fuel for the journey.

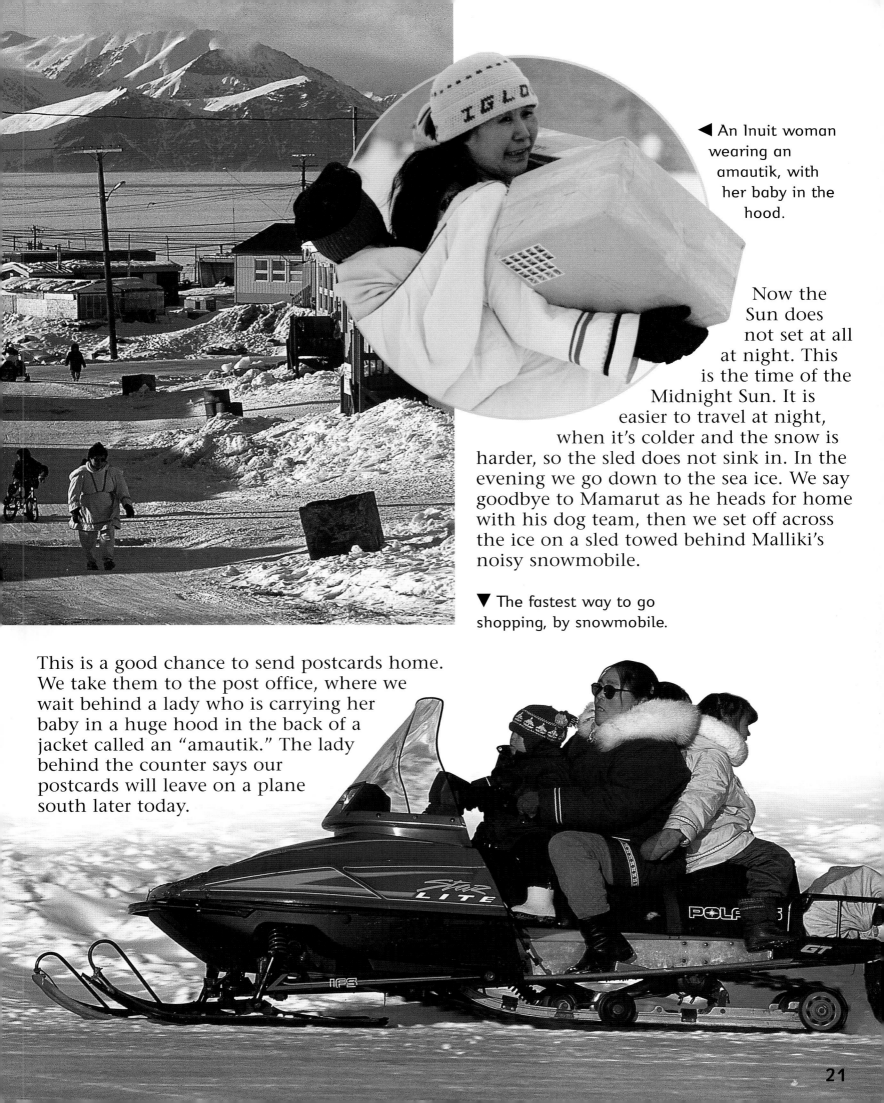

◀ An Inuit woman wearing an amautik, with her baby in the hood.

Now the Sun does not set at all at night. This is the time of the Midnight Sun. It is easier to travel at night, when it's colder and the snow is harder, so the sled does not sink in. In the evening we go down to the sea ice. We say goodbye to Mamarut as he heads for home with his dog team, then we set off across the ice on a sled towed behind Malliki's noisy snowmobile.

▼ The fastest way to go shopping, by snowmobile.

This is a good chance to send postcards home. We take them to the post office, where we wait behind a lady who is carrying her baby in a huge hood in the back of a jacket called an "amautik." The lady behind the counter says our postcards will leave on a plane south later today.

The Inukshuk and the Owl

As we travel away from the village, the Sun is very near the horizon and the sky turns pink, but the Sun never actually sets. Riding on a sled behind the snowmobile is very different from riding behind the huskies. We are going much faster, so it feels much colder and we bounce over every lump in the snow.

▶ The female snowy owl has yellow eyes and more black feathers than the male.

We have been traveling for over an hour when Malliki stops his machine. He calls us over to take a look at something through his telescope. On the rather flat tundra stands something that looks like a man. "Who can it be?" asks Malliki. It seems a long way to come for a walk. "Perhaps it's a ghost," he suggests with a grin. We drive toward it to find out. Soon we can see the figure without the telescope. It stands motionless in the middle of nowhere, its arms stretched out straight, looking distinctly spooky.

We are a little frightened when suddenly a white shape rises from the top of its head and flies away. Malliki thinks this is very funny. As we get closer we realize that it isn't a man or a ghost, but a figure made of stone. Long rocks make its outstretched arms, and sitting on the ground behind it is a female snowy owl, who has been using the figure as a hunting post from which to pounce on lemmings.

▶ An Inuk steadies his telescope on the windscreen of his snowmobile.

▲ The Sun is close to the horizon as we see a snow-covered inukshuk.

The figure is called an inukshuk. The Inuit used to build them to help them drive caribou when they were hunting. The caribou would think there were lots of hunters, rather than just one or two. Malliki knew what it was, but he wanted to have some fun with us. As we drive away, the snowy owl flies back to the top of the inukshuk. She still has to catch her food.

Musk
Oxen

We continue traveling across the snow-covered tundra. Malliki knows a lake where we can catch some fish to eat, and we follow a river to find the lake. As we round a bend in the river, we see a herd of musk oxen. They are grazing, digging in the snow to find grass under it. They have long coats that blow in the wind, and huge horns that meet across the front of their heads. There are young calves with them so they run away from us, their long fur swinging as they go.

▼ A herd of musk oxen stands facing into the wind, their coats full of wind-blown snow.

Once they are a safe distance away they form a circle around the calves, lowering their heads and stamping their feet at us. Those huge horns are very good protection against wolves and bears, but no match for a man with a gun. Today we are going to eat fish, not musk ox, so we continue up the river.

◀ A musk ox bull watches from beside a rock. He is ready to charge.

▶ Catching fish through a hole in the lake ice takes practice.

When we reach the lake it is covered with ice. How are we going to fish? Malliki uses a long steel pole to make a hole in the ice big enough to pull a fish through. He puts his fish hook and a shiny lure into the water, and wiggles it just below the surface. The fish are curious and come to the lure. When one grabs it, Malliki tugs the line and pulls the fish out of the water. Now we all have a try. It takes a little getting used to, but we all catch fish and soon we have enough for supper. After a good meal we put up our tents and settle down for the night. It's been an exhausting day.

Hunting
Caribou

W are woken by a snowmobile outside our tent. It is Jonas and his son, Levi. Over early morning tea they tell us they are going to hunt caribou, and ask us to join them. Jonas is teaching his son how to understand and respect the animals they hunt. It is important never to take too many animals, because if you kill them all, everyone will starve. To be a good hunter you need to know the places the animals like to be, and how to get close enough to shoot them without being seen.

We cross some caribou tracks, and Jonas shows us how to tell if they are fresh by the softness of the snow in them.

◀ Migrating caribou cast long shadows across their tracks in the snow.

26

These are very fresh, and by following them we soon find a small herd of caribou. Making sure that our scent is not carried to them on the wind, we stand and watch them. Jonas loads his rifle and hands it to Levi, who aims carefully at one animal. He wants to kill it quickly, with one bullet.

The shot is a good one. When the animal is dead, Levi helps his father to take off the skin. This will be used to make clothes. Levi is learning the lessons that he will need to live here as a hunter, to feed himself and his family off the land. We all share a meal of freshly boiled caribou, and before Jonas and Levi leave they give us another piece of meat. It is good to share with others when you have food so that later, if you are hungry, others will share with you.

▲ Caribou trot across a lake. Most of these are young animals, with small antlers.

◀ An Inuit hunter shows his son how to read caribou tracks in the snow.

▶ Skinning a caribou is skilled work.

27

From Winter to Summer

As we travel with Malliki, the days become much warmer. Now the temperature rises above freezing during the day. The snow on land is beginning to thaw, and the sea ice to crack. We are standing on the firm surface of the frozen sea when suddenly we hear a loud "thwack"! We watch as the gap, called a lead, in the ice between us and the snowmobile opens up.

We have to jump quickly over the open water to be on the same side of it as Malliki. That was close! Now as we travel, we often need to cross leads more than three feet wide. Malliki revs his engine and crosses the lead so fast that our sled doesn't fall into the water.

▲ The board at the front of the skis on this snowmobile stops the water from splashing up at the driver.

Now we are wearing rubber boots, because the water on the ice can be fairly deep in places and our warm footwear would get wet. Malliki uses a piece of wood on the skis of his snowmobile to stop the water splashing up at him.

► As the sea ice melts, this iceberg will be free to drift away.

▲ The icicles in this cave inside an iceberg are a spectacular sight.

▶ The noisy arctic tern hovers over us. Are we close to its nest?

We find an iceberg with a hole right through it. In this cave there are long icicles, created when the ice thaws during the day then freezes again at night.

Suddenly we hear the very loud call of a bird. A white bird, with a red beak and feet and a black cap, is hovering near us. It is an arctic tern, and it has just flown half way around the world. These little birds come to the Arctic in summer to breed, then, as winter approaches, they fly south again all the way to the Antarctic. This tern is one of the first of the Arctic's summer visitors.

Summer
Visitors

The Arctic summer is short. Once the thaw starts, it is a race against time. The plants do not have long to flower and make seeds, and the birds have only a few short weeks to build their nests, lay their eggs, and raise their young. But the seas around the Arctic are so rich in food that many birds travel north to make use of the long days and good food supply. The land animals will then feed on the eggs or young of the nesting birds.

▶ A large flock of gulls flies away from the iceberg they have been sitting on.

▶ A ptarmigan in its summer colors, which camouflage it as it sits on the nest.

We leave the snowmobile with a friend of Malliki's, and borrow a boat to continue our journey. There is still some sea ice, but it is now very thin. As we travel, we see lots of seagulls and other sea birds. On land the ptarmigan, which has been white all through the winter, is now a drab brown for camouflage, so you cannot see her sitting on her nest. Eider ducks line their nests with their own soft down feathers, to keeps their eggs really warm.

◀ The eider duck pulls downy feathers from her breast to line her nest.

We see a white gyrfalcon hunting along the cliffs. This large bird will soon have chicks of its own to feed. During the winter it eats mostly ptarmigan, but in the summer little auks, ducks, or gulls all make a good feed for its young.

◀ The white gyrfalcon preys on the wildlife of the Arctic.

Flowers,
Jewels of Summer

Malliki knows a place where the summer flowers are very good, so we pull the boat onto the shore and go for a walk. We look among the stems and flowers of the arctic willow to see if we can find any signs of a lemming.

The lemming is very important to many birds and animals in the Arctic. In years when there are lots of lemmings, owls and foxes manage to raise more babies. Lemmings are the fast food of the Arctic— the bottom of many food chains. Lots of animals depend on catching and eating them. We look carefully in the willow's twigs, as thick as our fingers. It is hard to believe that these willows could be hundreds of years old and yet so tiny.

◄ Brightly colored "pussy willows" are the summer flowers of the arctic willow.

We find some yellow arctic poppies. All their flowers are facing in the same direction, toward the Sun. Malliki explains that they turn their flowers in this way so that they can make the most of the 24-hour daylight and their seeds will ripen faster. They are also a welcome place for the flies that pollinate them to rest and shelter. Other flowers survive the cold by growing in low cushion shapes. They all need to set seed quickly in the short summer.

▲ Arctic poppies springing up on a stony beach, their yellow flowers turned toward the Sun.

▶ Purple saxifrage is the first plant to flower in the Arctic summer. It has very sweet nectar we can eat.

We also come across a big clump of purple saxifrage. Malliki shows us how to pull off the flowers one at a time and suck the tiny drop of nectar from the back of the flower. It is very sweet but there isn't much of it. It is probably a big meal for a lemming, though.

Time is running out for us too, and we need to get going. It was a shame we didn't see a lemming!

33

The tents are easy to put up and take down, which is good because the Nenets are nomads and travel long distances. As they gather round to welcome us, we are even joined by one or two young reindeer calves. We are made welcome in the tent of the Hudi family and Malliki says goodbye and returns to the boat; he has a long journey home. The floor is covered with reindeer skins. Hanging from the roof is a wooden cradle with a sleeping baby in it.

◀ A Nenets girl puts a harness on a reindeer that will be pulling a sled.

▶ A Nenets mother comforts her baby. The cradle is hanging from the top of the tent.

A Reindeer Herders' Camp

After a very long trip across the Arctic Ocean we arrive at the coast of Siberia. We walk a short way inland, to a Nenets reindeer herders' camp. Here we find a line of teepee-shaped tents surrounded by reindeer. Each tent, which is made from wooden poles and covered in canvas, houses one or two families.

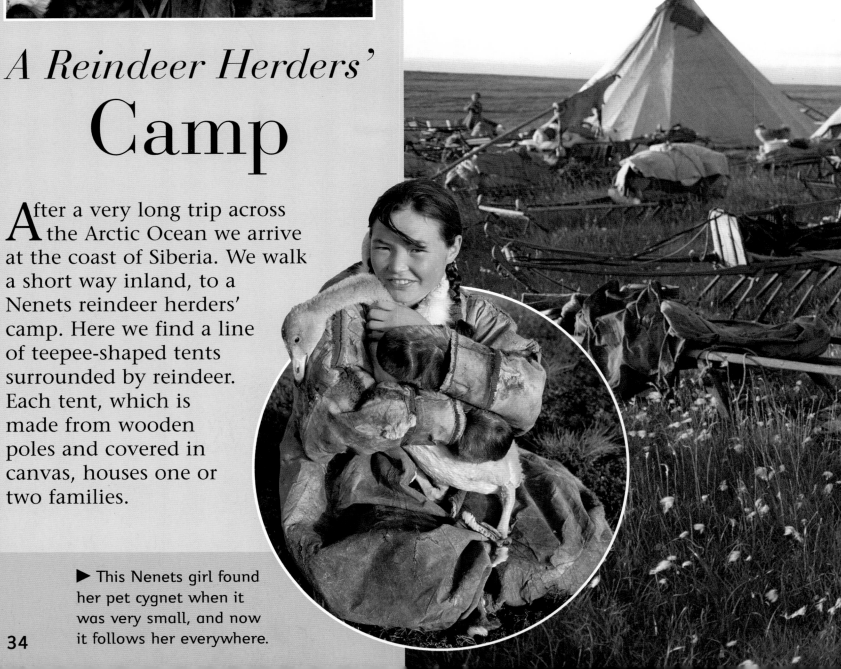

▶ This Nenets girl found her pet cygnet when it was very small, and now it follows her everywhere.

While we drink tea and eat raw fish and reindeer meat, Tanya Hudi explains that her family is on a long migration, following its reindeer. Each year they will travel 624 miles from the winter pastures to the summer pastures, then back again. We have met up with them during their return trip south.

The Nenets have a very close relationship with their reindeer, and give each one a name. Their survival depends on these animals—they use the skins for their clothing and tents, and eat the meat nearly every day of the year.

▼ Nenets tents at a camp on the summer tundra.

▲ Reindeer with velvety antlers pull the sleds across the lush grasses of the summer tundra.

A Reindeer
Sled Trip

A Nenets tent is a cozy place to sleep, and when we wake, the women are already up and busy, boiling kettles and packing up. Today we will be moving camp, so everything must be packed onto sleds. Very few people use sleds to travel on grass, because they work better on snow, but the Nenets' summer sleds are lighter than their winter ones.

Both male and female reindeer have been growing their antlers all summer, and now they are fully grown, with a soft covering of velvet. Soon they will harden and the velvet will peel off to leave hard, pointed antlers. The summer offers the reindeer a chance for good grazing on rich grasses and plants. The feet of both reindeer and caribou make a clicking noise when they walk, and now as we sit on the sleds we can hear it clearly. The group moves slowly, with between three and five reindeer pulling each sled across the soft, boggy ground.

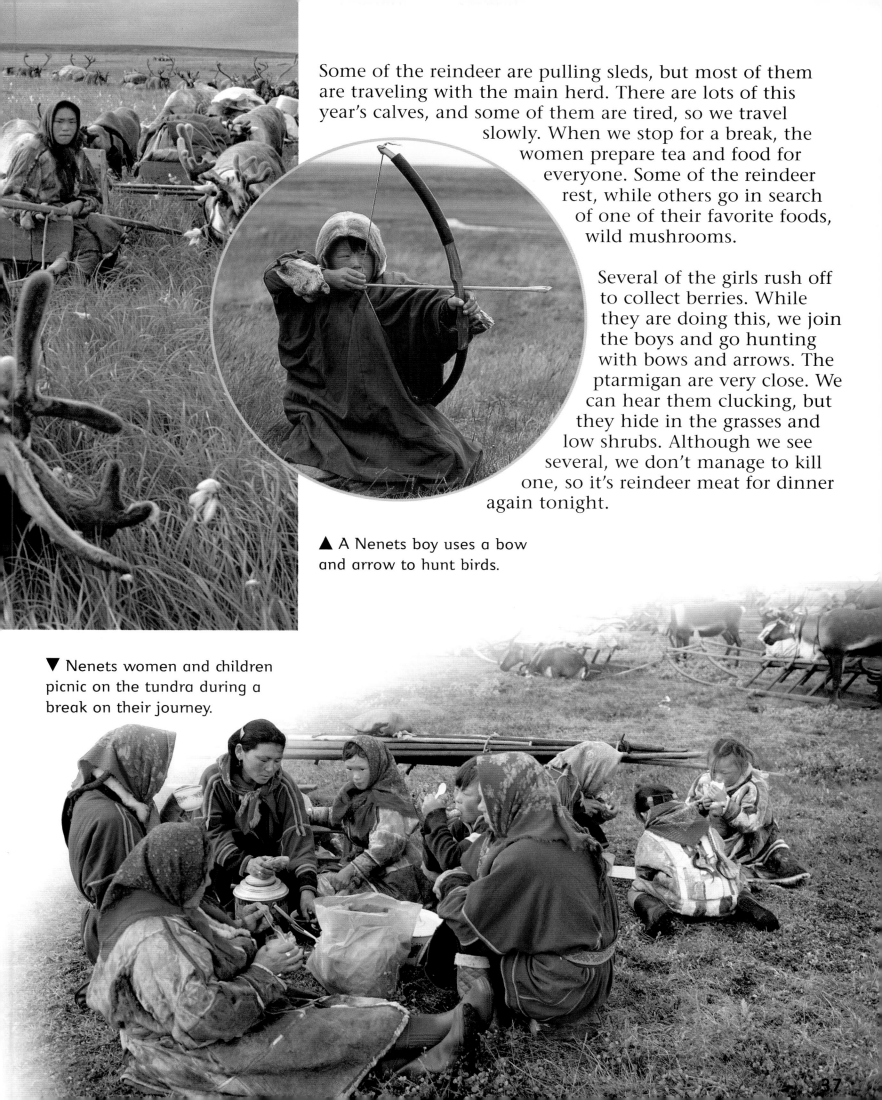

Some of the reindeer are pulling sleds, but most of them are traveling with the main herd. There are lots of this year's calves, and some of them are tired, so we travel slowly. When we stop for a break, the women prepare tea and food for everyone. Some of the reindeer rest, while others go in search of one of their favorite foods, wild mushrooms.

Several of the girls rush off to collect berries. While they are doing this, we join the boys and go hunting with bows and arrows. The ptarmigan are very close. We can hear them clucking, but they hide in the grasses and low shrubs. Although we see several, we don't manage to kill one, so it's reindeer meat for dinner again tonight.

▲ A Nenets boy uses a bow and arrow to hunt birds.

▼ Nenets women and children picnic on the tundra during a break on their journey.

Netting
Fish

We make camp that evening by a small lake. We will stay here for two days, to give the reindeer a chance to rest after the long day of travel. It also gives us a chance to set some nets to catch fish in the lake. They will be a welcome change from reindeer meat.

▼ A Nenets man checks one of the ropes on his fishing net.

▶ This boy's father caught this good-sized fish in his net.

The men set the nets across part of the lake, and leave them all night. Everyone has jobs around the camp: there are sleds to be repaired and skins to be sewn.

The children play games. Some of the boys pretend to be reindeer while we try to lasso them. Then we set off across the tundra, to collect firewood and berries. Some of the girls stay behind to help their mothers clean reindeer skins. This is the time when the women sew reindeer skin clothing for the coming winter.

We are eager to see what has been caught in the net, but the men tell us we must wait until after breakfast. At last we go to the lake. We see some of the floats bobbing up and down in the water, so we must have caught something. There are several big fish in the first net, but the second one is empty. We carry the fish back to the camp.

▲ Supper cooks in a pot hanging over a fire in the tent.

▶ A shy Nenets girl wraps herself in the fabric of her family's tent.

Polluting
the Arctic

Our journey the next day takes us past a place where they are drilling for gas. The work spreads over a large area, and broken machinery and trash litter the tundra nearby. We guide our reindeer past it as quickly as we can, so they do not cut their feet on sharp metal or get caught in wire.

▲ Summer pack ice melting in the Arctic Ocean.

It is easy to imagine that the Arctic is a pristine, white environment. But that isn't really true any longer. The things that we do in the towns of the south pollute the north. The winds that blow around the Earth pick up pollution from our industrial cities and carry it to the Arctic.

◀ Sparks fly at a copper foundry at Norilsk, Siberia, Russia.

▶ An oil spill from leaking pipes pollutes a lake near Niznevartovsk, Khanty Mansiysk, Siberia, Russia.

Global warming is affecting the whole world. There is 6 percent less sea ice in the Arctic now than there was 20 years ago. If this continues, life will become very difficult for animals like the polar bear that rely on hunting on sea ice to survive. Polar bears are also badly affected by toxins, or poisons, in the environment. When they eat other animals, they collect the toxins from them in their own bodies, and many are now very polluted.

Some places in the Arctic produce their own pollution. In the Russian Arctic, leaks from oil drilling are common. Where these happen, the vegetation is killed and lakes and rivers are polluted, with awful results.

We must hurry past the drilling rig, because we have to catch a helicopter flight later in the day, and we mustn't be late.

▼ Nenets herders drive their reindeer sleds past the gas exploration fields in their summer pastures.

Across the Arctic Ocean

We wave goodbye to our Nenets friends as the helicopter takes off. It will carry us 6 miles out to a Russian nuclear icebreaker, which is waiting in deeper water. The helicopter is noisy and shakes a lot, but it is wonderful to see the coast from the air. Landing on the back deck of the icebreaker is very exciting; from the air it does not look big enough to hold us.

We will travel due north on the icebreaker. Only a nuclear-powered ship is strong enough to break through the very thick pack ice. While we are in the strip of open water close to the coast, we see lots of birds flying past, mostly gulls and terns but some groups of little auks. They are feeding well before they migrate south. Suddenly a killer whale surfaces close to the ship, and blows a plume of water into the air as it breathes out! Birds and mammals alike are making the most of the plankton and fish in the Arctic waters.

▼ We sometimes see walruses hauled out on an ice floe in open water.

▲ A Russian MI-2 helicopter flying over sea ice in the Arctic Ocean.

► A polar bear walking on summer sea ice, which is covered with pools of water.

When we reach the ice and start forcing our way through, it takes a little while to get used to the noise of the floes scraping against the ship's hull. Sometimes the whole ship shudders when we hit some very thick ice. The captain sends an ice pilot up in the helicopter, to help us find a route through the pack ice.

Now we are so far north we see fewer birds and no whales at all. We do spot two polar bears, but our icebreaker frightens them and they run away. We have disturbed their hunting.

43

At the North Pole

It is hard to sleep with the Sun shining in through your porthole all night, but it is very far from warm here. When we step out on deck in the morning, there is white sea ice in every direction as far as we can see. The icebreaker crunches through it, leaving a dark trail of open water behind her.

◀ The Russian nuclear icebreaker *Sovetskiy Soyuz* crashing through thin summer ice on her way to the North Pole.

▶ The ice at the North Pole is constantly moving, so any sign will only be in the right place for a few minutes, before it drifts south.

This far north there is not much wildlife, but as we near the North Pole a single, pure white bird flies overhead. It is an ivory gull. It flies around the ship to get a good look, then flies on. The captain and crew are very excited, as very few people get to visit the North Pole. When the ship's Global Positioning System reads 90 degrees north, we are exactly at the Pole! The captain sounds the ship's horn and everyone cheers. A gangplank is lowered and a sailor puts up a North Pole sign.

NORTH POLE

NEW YORK
5,461 Km

LONDON
4,292 Km

ROME
5,439 Km

MOSCOW
4,348 Km

SOUTH POLE
20,000 Km

We take a short walk to get away from the ship, to feel the silence and think of the explorers who risked their lives and traveled for months in awful conditions to be where we are now standing. Many of them failed to get this far.

Some very hardy Russian sailors are swimming in the open water behind the ship! If we walk away from the sign in any direction, we will be walking south. We all join hands around the sign, and dance around the top of the world!

◄ The water is 30 degrees F, but does not freeze because of the salt in it.

Glossary

amautik Traditional woman's overgarment, with a large hood used to carry a baby.

Antarctica The polar region opposite the Arctic, occupying the extreme southern part of the Earth.

Arctic The cold area at the top of the world, north of the Arctic Circle.

arctic fox A small white or sometimes grey fox that lives in the Arctic.

arctic tern A small seabird that makes an extraordinary migration, breeding in the Arctic and flying to Antarctic waters to feed during the Arctic winter.

auks A group of seabirds that "fly" underwater and breed in the north.

bird of prey A bird that kills other birds or animals for food.

camouflage Fur or feather color that helps a creature hide.

caribou A member of the deer family, called reindeer in Europe; both males and females grow antlers.

conservation Protecting the natural world, including animals and the places in which they live.

cygnet A baby swan.

down Soft underfeathers on a bird; also the baby coat of a newly hatched bird.

ecosystem The way that all living things in an area live together and depend on each other.

eider duck A large sea duck with soft underfeathers.

food chain The line of connection between the smallest creatures that are eaten by bigger ones that in turn are eaten by even bigger ones.

glacier Slow-moving river of ice, formed by snow gathering on higher ground.

global warming Worldwide temperature rise caused by human actions.

gyrfalcon A white bird of prey that lives in the Arctic.

habitat The natural home of a plant or animal.

husky A strong dog with a thick coat, used to pull sleds over snow.

iceberg Large floating block of ice that has broken off a glacier.

icebreaker A ship with a strengthened hull that can be used to break up sea ice.

ice cap Large sheet of permanent ice on the land.

ice floe A floating slab of sea ice, not attached to land or other ice.

icicle Downward-pointing spike of ice made by thawing and refreezing.

igloo Inuit word for a house.

Inuit The name that the peoples of Canada and Greenland use for themselves in preference to the word Eskimo.

Inuk The word that the Inuit use for one Inuit.

inukshuk Meaning "like a man," the name given to stone figures on the tundra.

ivory gull Pure white gull found in the north and around the sea ice.

killer whale Black and white toothed whale.

lead Crack or break in sea ice.

lemming Small mouse-like animal that lives in the Arctic.

lure Something that flashes on the end of a fishing line to attract fish to the hook.

Midnight Sun The time in the summer when the Sun doesn't go below the horizon at night.

migration Movement of animals from one place to another, often related to the seasons and availability of food.

musk ox Long-haired herd animal that has big horns and eats grass, found in the Arctic.

nectar Sweet liquid found at the base of some flowers.

nomad Person who travels from place to place, often following animals as a hunter or a herder.

North Pole Imaginary point on the top of the globe where the lines of longitude meet.

pack ice Mass of floating pieces of sea ice.

plankton Tiny life forms, both animal and vegetable, floating in the sea.

polar Relating to the Arctic and Antarctica.

polar bear Large white bear that lives in the Arctic.

pollinate To transfer pollen from one plant to another to produce seeds.

pollution Spoiling the natural clean state of a place.

predator A creature that kills and eats others.

prey An animal that is hunted by a predator.

ptarmigan A bird of the grouse family that has white feathers in winter as camouflage.

reindeer A member of the deer family, called caribou in North America.

ringed seal A small member of the seal family, very common in the Arctic.

sastrugi Waves on the surface of snow caused by the wind.

saxifrage A kind of plant that grows in the Arctic and up mountains.

sled A snow vehicle with runners, which can be pulled across snow behind dogs or a snowmobile.

snowmobile A motor vehicle used in the Arctic; it has two skis at the front and can carry two people.

snowy owl A white owl that nests on the ground in the Arctic.

teepee Conical tent made from canvas or skins over poles, used by North American Indians.

toxin Poison.

tundra Treeless area in the north, where the soil is frozen just below the surface.

walrus A large member of the seal family; both males and females have ivory tusks.

Index

Acknowledgments

All photographs by Bryan and Cherry Alexander, except pages 32–33 (main picture), Hans Jensen Assilissokssuaq.

Artwork on pages 4–5 by Sarah Young.